Walking Here

JESSIE LENDENNIE

salmonpoetry

Published in 2011 by
Salmon Poetry
Cliffs of Moher, County Clare, Ireland
Website: www.salmonpoetry.com
Email: info@salmonpoetry.com

ISBN 978-1-907056-84-0

COVER IMAGE: *Jessie Lendennie*
COVER DESIGN: *Siobhán Hutson*

PRINTED IN IRELAND BY GEMINI

Salmon Poetry receives financial support from The Arts Council

for Eve

Acknowledgements

Thanks are due to the editors of the following where some of these poems appeared:

Stand Magazine, The Midland Review, The White Page / An Bhileog Bhán: Twentieth Century Irish Women Poets, Joan McBreen, editor (Salmon, 1999), *The Great Book of Ireland, The Echo Room, Dogs Singing: A Tribute Anthology* (Salmon, 2010) and *Shine On* (Dedalus Press, 2011).

A special Thank You to Philip Fried, Devon McNamara, Lex Runciman, and Ron Houchin for their astute editorial assistance. Thanks as well to Jean Kavanagh and, as always, to Siobhán Hutson.

Contents

For you, as always,
I'm not afraid of the dark anymore
I'm not forgetting
It's just that I've moved
And the light shifted

Notes from Home

1.

The usual woodframe house
The landowner a walk away
Across the cotton fields
Rumours of snakes
Under the porch
Lumber yard smell
Winter baths in the kitchen tub
Rain, wind, light
Mama, with no garden of her own,
Picking cotton

2.

Saturdays in town
A nickel for Woolworth's
Magpie finery
Kirby's drug store
Main Street Blytheville,
Following the rough sidewalk
To where it was paved
The good end of town

3.

And here I am again
In front of the only house
We ever owned
Green shingles warped
Screen door buckled
The house felt like
The neglected children I saw
Not my mother's children

Whose battles were outside,
Who pranced on the grass
Cheerleaders, Drum Majors

What would my mother have felt
The only house she ever loved
And Daddy, now another woman's landlord
In a dump in LA, dead drunk

4.

Suddenly there was my brother
Phoning from California
Years and distance, but
I knew him instantly
Because he said my name
The way I say it
But he was older alright,
And how did I sound
West coast with a difference
I didn't think to tell him
That there are palm trees here too
I have the advantage
I don't have to imagine him
In a California ranch house
We have more than a few in Ireland
But how is he to know?

So we talked about…. What?
The whys and wherefores of families
And we are like so many broken children
Grown into fractured lives

I hang up the phone
And he is someone who left me
And whom I left.

Promises

Do you remember my father who drank too much?
He made his sons take the Pledge
I didn't have to make promises
But ate chocolate and discovered junk food
At an early age.

And my mother...
Why didn't she leave him? Well
She'd known him so long – he was family
Not like the strangers I met
Who stayed strangers after years and years and years.

Blytheville

April 21st, 1988

In that heat
On the corner
Of Main Street
And Leclade
I knew I had
Not changed
Still felt
What I must feel
As if my very blood
Ran with that trickle
Of water in the ditch
Fell with the spare rain
On the hard earth
I was then
And I am now
Gypsy, Hobo,
Breathing the dry air
Lifting my arms
Like wings
Moving as if
The wind were rising
Above my home

Cotton

For my mother Willie Mae Harbin Lendennie

Would it have interested you to know
That cotton plants bloom in the valleys
Of the Amu Darya River?

You would remind me of cotton fields
Which stretched to the horizon
In the Mississippi Delta
When you were my age, with seven kids.
You would remember the way the men
Weighted the sacks, and the coins in exchange.

Now, without you, I am intrigued by names
Of places where cotton grows. So far away,
Like my early awareness of hot sun and sweat
And your broad-brimmed hat, above me.

Rain

1.

San Francisco rain
Up the hill to Bosworth Street
Lights on at 10am, shredding the mist
A child of rain knows the water
As it seeps from the sky
From the heart
Knows the sharp light of sun
On bottles broken in the street

2.

This is the Donegal sky
Translucent edges
East the clouds
Are a water fog
Swollen as if dripping inside
Water replacing itself
In ripples – wind layers
Over a grey restless lake
Cold grass twisting
Under a silver sky

3.

This window
One side yours,
One mine
I am as you
Lost in what was
Feel the ground shift
One more movement
Storms and stone walls
Edge the day

Galway Haiku Sequence

Above the old city wall
A circling seagull —
Watching the tide

The gull's cry
Louder than the wind
Against sails

Tourists at the docks
Shirts flapping
In a western wind

My desk, an exile voyage
Unopened
A letter from home

Between Us

for Michael

It is that Irish mid-August
So common now,
Wind holding the slanting rain
In place for hours

Then, sudden sunlight
As I watch your departing train
Moving along the Bay

I see how the sun shines
On this sleek silver water
A mirror of gulls

I wade in seaweed
Deep as an uncut field
And remember

You at King's Cross station
Riding the escalator backwards
And my son saying
"I know you miss him
when he's gone"

As if I never knew better
As if I never knew
Where we would be
These few years later

Parting on a day
When a sudden wind
Puts the sunlight
Between us

Yellow Weeds

Sun through the poor yellow weeds
Blue above the houses
And a wind
Sharp as a blade of grass

Stretched on this flat stone
In the half sun
Warmth before rain...
What did you say
That I believed
That now makes us
As separate as the wind
From this place

I am past caring
As if to say
"Look how this wall
Curves out
To scoop the bottom
From the sea".

Resurrection

In a pub in Galway,
Not quite the further reach
Of western civilization,
I nursed half a drink
For most of the night
And offered memories
To those too young
To reject them.

Someone had heard
That I was one of
Ingenious thousands
Who gathered to levitate
The Pentagon in 1967.
"Were you really *There*?"

How many lives have risen
Have fallen?

I am ancient beyond description
And something else
Long ago I gave up all belief
In resurrection.

Grattan Strand, Galway

Walking here
Has become my life
The air, the light
Clouds like the softest
Frosted breath,
The first autumn

I have been here
Long before the air
Smelt of change

And every mood
Has its vision
The horizon is both
This path
And the edge of the sea

And my life is bound
By every early morning
Wanting to be here
Wanting to be gone

Quay Street, Galway

There are ghosts on Quay Street
Not the Claddagh ghosts
Who looked for company
Late crossings on the bridge
To the old place
But my ghosts
Left behind on Fairhill
Wondering now where I am
Why the light flickered
Why I can't find my way home.

Zookie

The dog on the floor of the wine bar
Lifts her head at my apple pie and coffee
Sleeps again breathing to a country & western tune
She might be dreaming of chasing sticks
She might be dreaming of apple pie
Or the caress of sunlight on golden fur

I ignore the mirror's reflection
And the lopsided smile of the waitress

I want to lie on the floor in the sun
And chew sticks in my dreams
I want not to eat apple pie
On days when thoughts turn to fat

I want to talk with the dog
About philosophy, about fur
Ask her if she *likes* country & western
Ask her what I'm doing in this dark place
On a sunny day

I want to ask her why she waits for me

Gulls

1.

Christchurch, Dublin
And what moves me most
On this fair spring morning
Not the church bells, but
The sound of seagulls
For years they were my wake up
Call, across the Galway docks
Yet they stayed strangers to me
I don't know why they love cities
Or how they manage the sea
I only know that they gave my life
Meaning on the days when I woke up
Alone and listening

Gulls

2.

Jurys Hotel, Dublin
I chose the wrong room
Should have taken the
Church view
Instead opted for quiet
And got a back alley courtyard
Yet, I hear seagulls and
Their wild cries remind me
That on this bright day
In this half-strange city
I could walk to the river
Slowly find my way and walk forever
But this day is challenge enough, so
I'll stay quiet in the wrong room
Listening for the final call
Head bowed, wings tucked

Dublin

Can you be nostalgic for a place
You've never lived?
'Dublin in the rare ould times'
Poignant tune on early morning radio.
1979 Dublin empty streets
Ha'penny Bridge Bookshop –
Smell of discovery.
How can you live there and not live there?
Dublin was never my choice
Coming from London in search of space
And the clarity that defined poetry.
What did I see of Dublin then
Trinity College – rarified intellectual life
And a tight village of its own.
No, much earlier, with that 'Portrait…',
but I was never a young man
I was a girl in New York City
Troubled by a boy in that even rarer ould Dublin
Certainly not my times, never never my times.
Years later on O'Connell Bridge
I thought of that Liffey
How one image overlays another
The imaginative and the sensual
Here is recognition, here is, perhaps, reality.

Camera

I lost my camera in New York City,
46th Street, coming out of Carmine's
On my son's 40th birthday.
Photos of him, his dad, his aunt, my friend.
Left in the taxi, maybe dropped in the street
In the rush for the taxi
Too distracted to care much;
Get another camera,
There are other photos of the birthday.

Only, now I'm stuck,
Stuck with how then and now collide;
All those things I left behind
When I fled Manhattan decades ago,
All the things I didn't care about.

Blocks from where my son was born
I lost my camera on his 40th birthday
Around the corner from my first room
In New York City I let go of my life
As I did then   As I will always

Shannon Airport

And then there was the time
When leaving meant arriving
When all that I had been was again,
Only better.
January. Reykjavik, Luxembourg,
Walthamstow. Old London,
Just changing, but grudgingly.
And wasn't the world young then
Because I was.
Wondering now, how are we who we are
And not the next stranger?
What does returning mean
For someone who can never leave?

Flying in November

In the sky now, and the thought goes on
Returning... Not returning
Belonging, not as if I'd always been
But as kindred on a journey
Going to visit a past which shaped me,
Which was me when I wasn't in another world.
How far back, and why?
When leaving was romantic,
On the road again.

And all it took was an open mind
And willingness to imagine.
Now Ireland from the air
Looks like the dreams one has
Of falling and drifting,
Clouds lifted by sun
Not magic, but promise of a sort.

Election 2008

And that morning when I was in London
For the first time in twenty years,
When I had gone back to say hello
To another life. To see if I was still
There somehow. I found that memory
Was turned on its head again
And the reasons I left America
Were finally purged from my life;
I was sixteen again, in one of those flashes
Which always leaves one gasping
With significance, or sadness.
And I remembered the aspirations
That were so exciting, had such promise,
Back round again, despite what prowls
In the dark.

Sliding

1.

5th November, 2008

TV above my hotel bed
5am London
Staring at the blank screen
Staring. Willing my friend to wake up
From her quiet sleep in the next bed
I could feel her breathing in the tiny room
When at last she stirred, a little movement
I punched the TV remote
Volume down, but there it was
LANDSLIDE
LANDSLIDE
I felt that landslide, for once, loving the word
Taking it for one meaning only
The idea that things were shifting,
But this time in a way we could follow
The light changing before our eyes
Here in a small room in a London hotel
I was an American for the first time in 40 years.
In the hotel coffee shop I didn't hide my voice
I took the congratulations as if by right,
As if I had run this long long race myself.

2.

July, 2011

And what is it now that dims the fire for us
Were we really all desperate enough to believe
That America would wake up with pixie
Dust sprinkled on every sidewalk, field, valley
Island and shore? 'This Land is *Our* Land' on
Every billboard. Mountains dancing and all ills
Forgiven? Didn't some of us just want
Someone who could take on our job
And *try* to make that difference? Time, now, for the reality
Of the world to wake us up to the challenge
Of ourselves. We won't be children again, running
On golden beaches; too late for that, my Dear Generation.
My Dear Comrades-in-Arms.

London, 1972

I thought that we
Were probably
In New York
And that I had just
Run up five flights
Of stairs
To see you
And we were talking
Of living
Somewhere else

Crystal Palace Park

It was the trees – huge, stippled with light
That made me think of the circles
Of poplars in Crystal Palace Park
When we lay there
In a space that was defined by what we
Thought of as our own precious time
When the wind talked
When the trees listened

Thicket Road, London 1981

In memory I sit in my room
Above the garden
Someone comes quickly up the stairs
And knocks at the door

Now that room is gone from me
That room an empty shell
Now only the wind knocking

Yet still my mind echoes "come in come in"
I am myself, as then,
With no understanding of place and time
With no promise of understanding

And I have the same thoughts
Although they are thin and wavering
Quietly I say "come in come in"
But no answer

Once there existed questions
Can I say I have too many answers
Or only nostalgia
Dreams stretched upon a memory
A certain small corner of garden
Where I gathered the withered roots of clichés
Fuel for the dying thoughts of my life.

Thicket Road, London, 2011

For Philippe

We went back even though you didn't want to
And stood across the street and looked at the house
Always a beautiful house, a beautiful street,
Glorious trees; now massive, looming,
Emphasizing change and fantasy.
Old friends now, we stood in front of the place
That held us when we thought we were grown up
Where so much had happened with people
Whose names we can't completely remember
People who were so profoundly *us*,
A 70s commune that wasn't really a commune
With free spirits who played at being free
Who cried and laughed at once and pretended
Wisdom came with letting go of everything
Till then. And you were full of philosophy
And changed my life totally, utterly.

We stood across the street on a sunny May morning
And I thought of when I first met you, opening the kitchen door,
And all the open doors afterward; of my little Tim
In Crystal Palace Park, looking for tadpoles,
Of beautiful Maunagh skipping down the tall steps,
Of Bonita's sculptures, of Royston banging on the broken piano,
Of Lorenzo who befriended pigeons and was the only one
Courageous enough to take the ill and sad black dog for his last walk,
Of Simon, who was so disappointed in me.
Of everyone in and out of the rooms and doors; moving in
Moving on.

And every image, every second, tumbled into me, into us,
On Thicket Road that May morning. Here again.
And memory is a fracturing, a breaking of light and dark
It isn't that I am trying to return, only trying to see
What never left, yet still came with me.

North

Quiet on this Alaskan night
No lights over the icy sea, yet
The frozen land still calls a name
No one answers. Still climbs a hill
With no vision.
The voice of sea and land –
Only our own myth
Our own self-undoing

Wild

Years I spent looking for wilderness,
Searching.
Does that even make sense?
And where is it when you find it?
That wild – ness?
On the other side of the highway?
Across that stretch of meadow?
The top of that mountain?
Would you cross a river to get there, a lake; an ocean?
Go into the deep trees where the worn path fails?
Is that a kind of wild thinking
Or just another striving?
Would I really walk into those dark woods
And call out the wild
Maybe live maybe die.

Anchorage

And when you get off the plane
And the air is so icy
You can barely breathe
But so invigorating you're instantly high
Out of body with the purity of it all
And the streets
Wide like highways
Waiting for something to fill them
And you want to be part of this
Whatever it is that moves the light
That brings the snow

Wasilla

Eagles over an April lake
Near the shopping mall
At the guest lodge
In Wasilla
I felt loneliness like
Places that don't want to be found
The cabin that I wanted to buy
Faced the lake, away from the good road
And the dog tied in the yard
Felt desperate, recognized it in me
And something was wrong
Or going wrong.

Hope

Where I wanted to stay
Curled up by the fire
In the Hope Café
Beyond reach of irony
Buy a crazy-crooked house
With stilts for its foundation
Walk the wide street everyday
With an old dog who
Knows all the secret places
Live on the strength of neighbours
Learn how deep the snow lies
How the nights pass
How the summer begins
How it ends

Homer

Homer, Alaska
No ancient journeying, but
Down the unpaved road to the calm bay
I found a fresh way to see the world
A late sun slanted across the porch
Of the pristine cabin gallery
And of the coffee shop
Where I talked dog-years
As a way of belonging

April mix of heat and ice
I breathed deep to keep the images in
Pictures that may not mean anything
Anywhere else,
But I believe in the colour
Of this light, brushing
Along this street
Thick as toffee
Burnished as fine gold
Cherished as an ancient gift
In the strong sweet evening.

Spruce Island

for Carolyn

Flying onto Spruce
We skimmed low-lying clouds
And float-hopped along the bay
The arrival low key
No welcome
Just the exhilarating
Icy blast of adventure
We hiked up
To the makeshift cabin
Broke the lock
Having forgotten the key
(No matter here)
Lit the fire
A soft snow
Drifted over from Kodiak
This is your place now
She said
Let me show you
And we walked
This is where your land starts
This is where it ends
No one else within sight.
What I wanted
Didn't want
Wasn't sure.
I could stay here
Yes, happily,
With the spirit
Of Father Herman
Who lived on the island
For 40 years
Who helped the islanders
Always, whose

Followers kept trying
To build a church for him
But never succeeded.
The island, haunted.
I could live here. I could.
Bringing water over from Kodiak
Taking the boat instead
Of the float plane to save money
Stocking up on provisions
Walking the 12 miles up the island
To the community of Ouzinke
I could try, I could, to become
Part of something Sacred

Leaving, there were Salmon
In a small stream
That rolled down to the beach
Beautiful Salmon
Going home or starting out,
I had no idea.

Kenai Peninsula

I saw a black bear at last
A young one
Not so many around
So I was lucky,
But it was only a glimpse
Before he scrambled away.
An hour more of walking
Took me round the grounds
Of the new hotel
Spread out like a campus
With apartments
Smelling of fresh wood
And luxury
The suite way too big
For one person,
But there I was, alone,
Dozing finally, and
The voice of the bear when it came
Was the voice of a young man
A spirit from the dark woods
Ordering me out
With the hatred
Of those conquered
By this pretty hotel
By this too-big bed
No matter that I said
It wasn't me
It wasn't me

Poets in Cafés in Talkeetna

for Ron, Michael & Tom

Always cafés, and such wonderful coffee in Alaska,
The secret is keeping it cold.
Always getting a sense of the place from who's there, who's not.
When there are guns on the wall, that says something,
But maybe not what you think, or want them to say.
No stuffed heads, so open to interpretation
Laughing about that on an afternoon away from
Putting names on everything.

Atlin, Northern British Columbia

Smoke from forest fires
On the far side of Atlin Lake
And at the perfect harbour
Boats and float planes rock in the mist
Like their people, knowing the shift
Between danger and what is simply
Another summer day.
I found an old fisherman's house
That felt like I had just left it
So familiar it would make anyone
Believe in past lives.
And I wanted to sit and wait
For everyone to come home.

In the morning light, beyond the smoke
I walked and thought of how
This far place could be
So full of my memories
So full of beautiful women
Who owned the land; who walked proudly
Whose silver dogs ran in the sea, unhindered.
Who made their own lives
I thought of why I couldn't stay
I thought of why I had to leave.

Skinny D's

For Jerah

Between Anchorage
And Fairbanks –
'Skinny Dick's Half Way Inn'
With Skinny Dick's own brand
Of Alaskan rough.
I wanted a sweatshirt
But hung back a bit
Talking to a comfortable
Old dog on the wide front porch
Missing my own dogs
Who would have loved
Being here; being wild
For a time.
You came out, bags in hand
Smiling at a remembered joke,
Urging me to buy a shirt.

Inside, the shop was a cavern,
Massive, and on every surface,
Hanging from the ceiling,
Draped across furniture:
T-shirts and sweatshirts
Every colour, every size,
All displaying the same
central image.
Me and Skinny Dick
Alone in a cave
With copulating polar bears
Everywhere I looked
Polar bears were at it
On a sea of blue, green,
Orange, yellow,
Small, Large, XXL

XXL okay. Not one to
Back away from a challenge
I chose green. The
XXL bears smiled,
Looked happy.

My Curb in Eden

i.m. Joe Enzweiler

You were sitting at a corner table
At Into the Woods
Reading your poetry to local students,
I was drinking coffee and eating a gigantic
Genuine cinnamon bun, waiting for a friend
Who would introduce me to one of
Fairbanks' best loved poets
Who left his science career and built his own
Cabin years earlier, before it became less an escape
Than a fashion statement.
I knew, of course, that this must be you,
Curly hair tossed, lanky legs stretched
Inclining your head toward an important point
With the diffidence of a poet who lives his work,
Not totally sure of the effect of his voice.
I was smitten, yes, off again after another
Elusive poet. But no, this time it was about
the poetry. And when you caught my eye
I knew that's what would matter most of all.

Cabins

I've started looking at cabins again
Sitting at my desk
Gazing down the valley
To Liscannor, Lahinch
And the Bay
I've started thinking about cabins again
The house on the hill
The old cottage near the docks
Moved into memory
Even as I lived in them
I've started dreaming about cabins again
Walking the stones of Clahane
Looking out at the stretch of sea
Forgetting, for a moment, that I am
Slave to a metaphor for purity
In thrall to an image of freedom

Kinsale, County Cork, July

Mild and overcast at the docks
Bright edges give a sparkle to the clouds
A breeze made for daydreams
Drifts across the pale sea,
Settles at my dockside table.
And this is my alternative life —
Sipping coffee in outside cafés,
But I chose London over Paris
In 1970, that is, part of me did
The Paris-self recognizes
Breezy street life, small white dogs
Stuffy bookshops, Sartre and de Beauvoir
At a sideways table.
London was embankment walks
And wine bars in the rain
Afghan Hounds in Notting Hill Park
Unruly English days, and philosophy
Trapped on bookshelves.
Here, romantic Ireland smells
Of soft wind off the harbour
Feels like boats riding on upside-down clouds
Sailing, drifting, floating, flying
Life after life after life.

Flaw

I have descended into the body
Pain pulling me in
Calling me home
Now I am a living irony
So many years
Walking walking walking
Head high, thoughts swinging
Joking about getting old
And dying young
Now I am the joke
Now pain and I co-exist
She in the body I never knew I had
Me, struggling to keep up,
Trying not to look back,
Despising my dependence
The fatal flaw

Passage

Glasgow airport
Late, hurting,
Feeling the cold disinterest
And the crush of movement.
I move out of step
Break the flow
Forced to acknowledge
My steps as they
Weigh me down.
I move slowly and see
That I am among ghosts
Whose bodies are anywhere
But here in this uncertain place
A place that isn't a place
At all, but a testing ground
For what makes us human.
I am a ghost, too,
but out of time
I feel my legs
The ache in my knees
I could fall now, down and down
Out of time,
Right through that crack
In the dark passageway
Right through that crack
In the clouds

Hills

Can one be afraid of hills
Or is the fear more a fear
Of challenge. Of testing weak legs
Against the inevitable.
Finding, finally, that there are
Tasks you can't meet.

And what about the hills
That are personal.
That were once your friends,
It's a sad thing that they
Can't comfort you now.
That they turn their backs
And stretch up and you'll never again
See the city from the top of your climb
And you'll never know if the world
Above has changed
Nor even know if the world
Below still holds you.

Edge

Too many people
On this rocky strip of beach
Good for dogs
And okay for their companions
But why come out for sun
On this dim August day
When the sky
Is triple layered
And the slice of the wind
Leaves summer behind.
Me, I limp over stones
Trailing behind five dogs
Of varying speed.
None wait for me
But bolt for the nearest rock pool
Not stopping
But they do look back
As if I might lose
My place after all
Follow another pack
Maybe take a wrong turn
At the edge of the sea.

Invisible

"Old women are invisible,"
She said once
Flirting her way across America
Age 60. Still keeping men waiting,
She was not ready to let go of the girl
Who made men cry, men who begged
Her not to go.
But go she did, leaving friends as well as lovers.
For me she left a puzzle
I had no chance to agree or disagree
Somewhere, I'm certain, even in another life
She still moves gracefully, still flirts
With her invisible self.

4th August, 2011

Grim sky over the Cliffs
On this pale 4th of August
News of Italy's rumbling
Tumbling economy
That even Berlusconi's boogie
Can't fix, and, maybe doesn't
Want to fix. Who knows.
Spain spins by, engrossed
In the dance,
Past the resuscitation tent
Off to invite all of Europe
To the party.
Or so we are told.
And my beautiful Obama
Who shares this
Cloudy birthday with me
Seems to have tucked in his glorious
Lion's tail, and let the hyenas
Have the meat.
And I am finally sixty-five
And have been round and round
Like the old Kingston Trio song
About the guy on the Boston
MTA – round and round
The subway stops
Because he couldn't afford to get off
Maybe that was even
A comfortable life
Better than having one dream
After another fail on what
We thought of as the right road.
And in Ireland, daily murder
Mixes with meltdown. Quiet chaos
But no far-right fringe, no loud one anyway,

And the festivals keep celebrating
And the poets keep writing
As do I, even penniless
Even without assurance of any kind
Even if I reach the top of the hip
Replacement list after I'm dead
Even if my old hip, even if my sad knees
Go with me to the grave.

Pretty

When all you can do
Is remember that you were pretty once
And used it without even meaning to
And you only know this now because it's gone
Wherever these things go
The things that give a woman
A certain definition
Welcome or not.

When it doesn't matter
That memory is more important
Than waking each morning
When you want to go back
When you want to be pretty
Again and have all those years
When you couldn't possibly know
That someday it would matter.

West Coast

i.m. Carl Wilson

The usual cows graze on the hills outside my window
Rotating up and down; Bas-relief on big feet
The weather, as usual, is a sun that comes and goes
Flits across the valley without ceremony
Fifty years on and the Beach Boys stream out from the radio
Bringing that other West Coast right here to my sunless place
Hawthorne and chubby Carl Wilson in 6th grade
Spin-the-bottle parties and hide and seek
Figs rotting in back alleys in the ever-present heat
Another boring LA suburb sleeping before the world
Became a California surf
And, you could say, before the ocean became a metaphor
For escape, for our irreconcilable lives.

Knockeven, County Clare

This evening
Yellow-layered light drifts
Blue at the edges
Streaked grey above the sea
Deep blue falls across the field.
And the single ash tree
Stripped after the last storm
Has strong leaves again
Triumph over the searing wind.
Thistles reach across the yard
Bright yellow sparkles in the pale grass;
The indifferent wealth of growth,
Of storm and sun.

On my desk there are petals from the flowers
I bought to cheer the room, lying on the edge
Of the mosiac bowl. Red and yellow lilies
As bright as the tiny glass pieces
Placed to catch the light, when we have so little.
A kind of beauty in the close days,
Of storm and survival.

For the Guys with Apologies for Human Frailty

One dog under my desk
Another upstairs under the bed
Two outside on the soft gravel
And one on the scrunched-up rug

And I ask them:

Why? Why not me under the bed
And you at the desk?

But they don't want to trade down
And I can keep my species specific
Guilt trip to myself,
Thanks.

Keys

For Devon

Sudden rain streaks sideways
Across the valley, but the sun
Shines on the other side of the Bay.
West of Ireland weather, which I know
you'll miss. Last night there was
A huge rainbow almost upright.
I hope you saw it before you left.

And I find myself missing you
And smile again, at our rush back
To the beach to get the shopping
I thought I'd left there
But had already put away,
At the crush of dogs and women
In my crazy kennel-car
And the dogs so excited
To have you walking with us
And at the Stonecutter's Restaurant
Eating the best Banoffee ever created
In celebration of books and poems.
And you giving me the keys
To your cottage
"Will you remember what they're for?"

Will I remember?
The keys you lost
On the road to Liscannor
And found the next day
Tied to a fence just above
Where you'd dropped them.
The keys to a stretch of sea,
Stunningly blue in late summer
The keys to a perfect morning light

Across the Aran Islands
To a wave of late summer flowers
With Autumn coming on the wind.
The keys to a deep deep silence.

Yes, I'll keep the keys safe
And light the fireplace in the cottage
During the winter storms when sunshine
Will be a memory from another lifetime
And the gales tear across the sea.

Only, this morning there is a breeze
That lifts the light in the valley
And brings it, spinning, to me and I am
Caught, overtaken, by beauty. A beauty
That breaks the heart with the sadness of loss and change.
And my heart wishes that you were here to go walking
With me and the dogs and we could see things
As they should be, one and the other, and
I'll remember that I am only here through a kind
Of grace and I'll know that I can't always understand
And I will know that I can be happy with that.

Photo: Laura Lundgren Smith

JESSIE LENDENNIE was born in Blytheville, Arkansas. She left the US for London, England, in 1970. After ten years in London she settled in Galway, Ireland. Her previous publications include a book-length prose poem *Daughter* (1988); re-released as *Daughter and Other Poems* in 2001. She compiled and edited: *Salmon: A Journey in Poetry, 1981-2007* (2007); *Poetry: Reading it, Writing It, Publishing It* (2009) and *Dogs Singing: A Tribute Anthology* (2010). She is co-founder (1981) and Managing Director of Salmon Poetry. Her poems, essays and articles have been widely published and she has given numerous readings, lectures and writing courses in Ireland and abroad, including Yale University; Rutgers University; The Irish Embassy, Washington D.C; The University of Alaska, Fairbanks and Anchorage; MIT, Boston; The Loft, Minneapolis, MN; Café Teatre, Copenhagen, Denmark; the University of Arkansas, Fayetteville; The Irish American Cultural Centre, Chicago and The Bowery Poetry Club, New York City. She is currently working on a memoir *To Dance Beneath the Diamond Sky*.